"From Couch Potato to Healing Potato" is a light-hearted and quirky self-help book that combines personal development with the wisdom of potatoes. With humour, wisdom, and playful insights, this book offers a unique journey of growth and self-discovery. Embrace your inner "Tater Tot" and find inspiration to sprout, flourish, and become the best version of yourself. This book is your passport to a world where personal development meets playful adventure.

To complement the book's journey, we also offer a
"Potato Eater's Diary" and a
"Spud Journal."
The diary allows you to record your daily adventures, challenges, and Tater Tot moments, while the journal provides a space for deeper self-reflection, gratitude, and creative expression. These companions let you dive even deeper into the spud-tacular world of personal growth while embracing the whimsical spirit of the book.

Within the pages of this delightful book, you will notice some blank pages, they are for your own potato doodles, musings and wisdom on your healing journey. Have fun, life is too short to be miserable.

Welcome to "From Couch Potato to Healing Potato."

My friend,

Congratulations on embarking on this unique and spud-tacular journey of personal growth and self-discovery! Within these pages, you'll find the quirky wisdom of potatoes woven into a tapestry of inspiration, laughter, and transformation.

Just like a potato, you have the incredible power to sprout, flourish, and become something extraordinary. Embrace your inner "Tater Tot" and discover the magic in every moment. This book is your passport to a world where personal development meets playful adventure.

As you turn each page, remember that every day is a chance to bring a different "Potato Dish" to the table. Whether you're seeking resilience, creativity, mindfulness, or simply a heaping serving of positivity, the healing power of the potato is here to guide you.

Get ready to peel back the layers of your true self, nourish your body and soul, and transform into the best version of you. Be encouraged to engage in the quirky challenges, embrace the spud-tacular mantras, and reflect on your personal growth with a playful twist.

Your journey starts here, and it's bound to be a mash-up of joy, discovery, and transformation. So, dive into the world of "Potato Zeniths" and set forth on your path from Couch Potato to Healing Potato!

With spud-tacular love and encouragement,

June Rose

From Couch Potato to Healing Potato

Index

Lesson 1: The Great Couch Caper: Potato's Awakening
Lesson 2: Spuds and Serenity: Mashing Up Mind-Body Magic
Lesson 3: Energize Like a Tater Tot: Unearthing Your Inner Energy
Lesson 4: Potato Peeling: Uncovering Your Inner Self
Lesson 5: Tater Transformation: The Potato's Healing Mindset
Lesson 6: Meditato-tion: Spud-tacular Mental Makeover
Lesson 7: Munch Your Way to Healing: A Potato's Guide to Nutrition
Lesson 8: Spud Squats and Potato Planks: Spud-tacular Movement
Lesson 9: Breathe Like a Potato: The Art of Tuberous Tranquillity
Lesson 10: Emotion Fries: Crispy, Crunchy Emotional Healing
Lesson 11: Spud-uality: Finding Zen in Potato Zeniths
Lesson 12: Tater's Toolkit: Whacky Healing Wonders
Lesson 13: Potato in the Park: A Picnic with Nature
Lesson 14: Friendship Fries: How to Ketchup and Heal
Lesson 15: Mashed Missions: Uncovering Your Life's Butter Purpose
Lesson 16: Heal and Peel: Potato's Guide to Creative Cuisine
Lesson 17: Baked Battles and Fried Fiascos: Overcoming Challenges
Lesson 18: Spud Rituals: Tuber-Therapy for Everyday Life
Lesson 19: Potato Gratitude: Give Thanks, Not Starches
Lesson 20: From Spud to Superhero: Your Healing Journey Continues

Lesson 1:
The Great Couch Caper: Potato's Awakening

From Couch Potato

To Healing Potato

In a world not so far from your living room, there lived a mighty couch potato named Pam. Pam was the epitome of someone stuck in a comfort zone so deep that even the most enticing bag of cheese and onion crisps couldn't lure her away. But little did she know that her life was about to take a tuber-tastic turn.

Picture this: Pam, draped in her comfiest pyjamas, a remote control in one hand, and a bag of smokey bacon crisps in the other, blissfully lost in the depths of her squishy couch. She was so skilled at binge-watching TV that she could predict the next plot twist before it even happened. Okay, not really, but she wished she could!

One fateful evening, as Pam was about to embark on yet another Series marathon, a peculiar thought sprouted in her mind like a rogue potato vine. "Am I really making the most of my time on this planet?" she wondered, crumbs of doubt falling from her crisp-covered chin.

And so began The Great Couch Caper! Inspired by this newfound curiosity, Pam decided it was time to dig herself out of the proverbial couch cushions and embark on a journey of self-discovery, healing, and epic potato proportions.

This isn't just about Pam's quirky adventures; it's about your awakening too! You see, Pam's awakening is a metaphor for anyone who's been stuck in a rut or a comfort zone. It's for those who have wondered whether there's more to life than being a certified couch potato.

So, *my friend*, if you've ever felt like Pam, it's time to grab your spud spirit and join us on this peculiar, fun-filled, and informative adventure. Together, we'll explore the uncharted territory beyond the couch, where you'll learn how to awaken your inner potato and transform into a spud-tacular version of yourself.

Like a Potato

I find strength in the dark

Let the caper begin

Lesson 2:
Spuds and Serenity:
Mashing Up Mind-Body Magic

As Pam embarked on her journey to awaken from her couch potato slumber, she quickly realised that it was more than just a change in scenery; it was a quest to harness the magical powers of the mind and body. It was time to mash up some mind-body magic, and what better guide than the humble spud?

Pam's first lesson on this enchanting journey was all about serenity. You see, she had the TV at full blast, crisps crunching, and a storm of thoughts racing through her head. Serene wasn't exactly in her vocabulary, but she was eager to learn.

Our quirky guru on this leg of the adventure was none other than

"Sereni-Tater,"

a wise potato who radiated peace like a meditation guru.

Sereni-Tater taught Pam the art of stillness, starting with a challenge: "Pam, see if you can sit quietly for just five minutes."

At first, this seemingly simple task felt as challenging as walking on hot coals. Pam squirmed, fidgeted, and even contemplated going back to her trusty couch. But she persisted, focusing on her breath and learning to be present in the moment.

Before she knew it, Pam was experiencing the serenity she had only dreamed of. She was amazed at how five minutes of quiet contemplation could calm her inner storms. And so, she graduated from the

"Spud School of Serenity" with flying colours.

But the lesson didn't end there. Pam was introduced to the magical world of mindfulness, where every bite of a savoury potato crisp could become a transcendent experience. **Sereni-Tater** encouraged Pam to savour each crisp, to feel the texture, taste the flavours, and embrace the moment.

Mindfulness is all about being fully present and aware in the moment. It means paying attention to your thoughts, feelings and surroundings without judgment. It's like taking a mental step back to observe your experiences without getting lost in them. By practicing mindfulness, you can reduce stress, improve focus and gain a deeper understanding of yourself. Its like giving your mind a little holiday from the chaos of everyday life to simply be in the here and now.

By the end of this lesson, Pam was no longer just a couch potato; she had graduated to become a mindful masher, someone who could find serenity in stillness and joy in the little things.

Now, *my friend*, it's your turn to mash up some mind-body magic. Find your own **"Sereni-Tater"** within you and discover how serenity and mindfulness can transform your life, one magical moment at a time.

The adventure continues!

Lesson 3:
Energize Like a Tater Tot:
Unearthing Your Inner Energy

After Pam's enlightening journey into the realm of serenity, she felt a newfound sense of calm and clarity. But as she continued her quest, she discovered that there was more to life than just relaxation; she needed to energize like a tater tot!

Pam's next quirky guide on this adventure was none other than

"Ener-G-Tater,"

a potato with boundless enthusiasm and energy.

Ener-G-Tater was known for bouncing off the walls, or in this case, the potato fields, with uncontainable vigour. Pam couldn't help but be intrigued.

The first lesson from **Ener-G-Tater** was that energy wasn't something you could buy in a can; it was something you could cultivate from within. So, Pam, the former couch potato, learned that unearthing her inner energy began with a few potato-inspired practices.

Potato Power Snacking:
Ener-G-Tater introduced Pam to the magic of healthy snacking. While the savoury crisps were still on the menu, Pam discovered the wonder of energizing snacks like sweet potato fries, avocado toast, and the all-mighty potato salad. She soon realized that these spud-tacular bites not only satisfied her taste buds but also fuelled her energy levels.

Dance Like No One's Watching:
Ener-G-Tater encouraged Pam to find her inner groove and dance like a tater tot. Whether it was the mashed potato dance or her own funky moves, Pam discovered that dancing released endorphins, giving her a burst of natural energy.

Sprint and Rest:
Ener-G-Tater explained that life was all about sprints and rests. Just like a potato plant needs time to grow and rest, Pam needed to balance her activities with periods of relaxation. Pam was surprised to find that her energy levels soared when she respected her body's need for rest.

By the end of this lesson, Pam was no longer just a couch potato; she had become an **"Ener-G-Tater"** who could tap into her inner energy reserves whenever she pleased.

Now, *my friend*, it's your turn to embrace your inner tater tot and unearth your inner energy. No matter your starting point, you can learn to cultivate a spud-tacular source of vitality that will help you tackle life's adventures with gusto.

The journey continues with more potato-fuelled wisdom and whimsy!

Lesson 4:
Potato Peeling:

Uncovering Your Inner Self

As Pam continued her whimsical adventure, she found herself on a path of self-discovery. It was time to peel back the layers of her own life, much like the layers of a potato, and uncover her inner self.

For this part of her journey, Pam's guide was

"Peel-O-Tater,"

an expert in unearthing the true essence of a potato and revealing the beauty beneath the surface.

With her trusty peeler in hand, **Peel-O-Tater** showed Pam how to embark on her own potato peeling adventure.

The Outer Peel:
Just as a potato has a protective outer layer, we often wear metaphorical "masks" in our daily lives. Pam learned to identify the roles she played and the expectations she carried. She realized that peeling away the outer layers allowed her to be more authentic and connect with her true self.

Discovering the Core:
The heart of a potato is where the real magic happens. **Peel-O-Tater** explained to Pam that her core values, beliefs, and passions were like the potato's heart. Pam reflected on what truly mattered to her and what brought her joy.

Embracing Imperfections:
Potatoes, much like people, have imperfections. Some have blemishes or odd shapes, but they're still delicious. Pam understood that it was okay to embrace her quirks and imperfections. In fact, they were part of what made her unique and lovable.

Peeling Away Baggage:
Just as you can remove unwanted spots from a potato, Pam learned how to shed emotional baggage that was holding her back. She let go of past regrets and hurts, allowing her to move forward with a lighter heart.
Peeling away baggage is done by acknowledging and confronting the things that are bothering you or holding you back. You start by recognising what those emotional or mental burdens are, then you work on processing and letting go of them. This can involve talking to someone you trust, journaling or seeking professional help. It's like cleaning out your mental closet and tossing out the

things that no longer serve you, so you can make room for better things in your life.

By the end of this Lesson, Pam wasn't just peeling potatoes; she was peeling back the layers of her life to reveal her true self. She discovered that self-discovery was like uncovering hidden treasure, and it was a lifelong adventure filled with surprises.

Now, *my friend*, it's your turn to grab your peeler and join Pam and **Peel-O-Tater** on this quirky quest. As you embark on your own potato peeling adventure, remember that uncovering your inner self is a delightful and liberating process.

The journey of self-discovery continues with more spud-tastic insights and surprises!

Lesson 5:
Tater Transformation: The Potato's Healing Mindset

With newfound self-awareness from her potato peeling adventures, Pam was ready to dive into the heart of her transformation. It was time to cultivate a healing mindset that would not only change her life but also turn her into a true **"Tater Transformer."**

For this leg of her journey, Pam had a peculiar companion,

"Mindset Masher,"

a potato with an extraordinary ability to turn negative thoughts into mashed positivity.

With a potato masher as her magic wand, **Mindset Masher** helped Pam shape her way of thinking in a more spud-tacular direction.

Cultivating Positivity:
Pam quickly realised that negativity was like a rotten potato in her mental pantry. **Mindset Masher** taught her to replace negative self-talk with positive affirmations. For every "I can't," she mashed it into "I can!"

A Dash of Gratitude:
Pam started her day with a dash of gratitude, just as she'd sprinkle salt on her fries. **Mindset Masher** showed her that acknowledging the good things in her life, no matter how small, could have a magical effect on her outlook.

Seeing Challenges as Opportunities:
Just as a potato seed sprouts and pushes through the soil to reach the sun, Pam learned to see challenges as opportunities for growth. **Mindset Masher** encouraged her to tackle difficulties with a positive, can-do attitude.

Mental Hydration:
Just as potatoes need water to thrive, our minds need nourishment too. Pam discovered that feeding her mind with inspirational books, podcasts, and positive influences helped her maintain a healthy mental diet.

By the end of this Lesson, Pam had not only changed her outlook on life, but she had also transformed into a true **"Tater Transformer."**

She realized that the potato's healing mindset was not only about her own well-being but also about positively impacting the world around her.

Now, *my friend*, it's your turn to become a

"Tater Transformer."

With a healing mindset, you can turn life's challenges into opportunities and cultivate a positive outlook that will bring joy, resilience, and spud-tacular Magic into your life.

The journey of transformation continues with more potato-inspired wisdom and whimsy!

Lesson 6:
Meditato-tion: Spud-tacular Mental Makeover

Pam's journey of transformation was in full swing, and she had peeled away layers of doubt, nurtured a healing mindset, and was now ready for a spud-tacular mental makeover. This Lesson introduced Pam to the enchanting world of "Meditato-tion," a unique form of meditation guided by the wisdom of the potato.

Pam's meditation mentor was none other than

"Yogi Potato,"

a master in the art of stillness and mindfulness. **Yogi Potato** was a Zen master of the spud world, and his presence brought a serene, quirky energy to Pam's journey.

The Potato Pose:
Yogi Potato began by teaching Pam the art of the "Potato Pose." Instead of complicated yoga positions, they kept it simple. Sitting comfortably with her legs crossed, Pam imagined herself as a peaceful potato rooted in the Earth. This grounding visualisation helped her find inner stillness.

Meditato-chips:
Yogi Potato introduced Pam to "Meditato-chips," a practice where she focused on her breath, just as one would focus on the savoury flavours of a delicious crisp. With every inhale and exhale, she let go of stress and worries, allowing her mind to become as crisp and clear as a golden potato crisp.

Spud-tacular Visualisation:
Yogi Potato encouraged Pam to embrace the power of visualisation. She imagined herself as a thriving potato plant, absorbing nutrients from the Earth and reaching for the sunlight. This visualisation connected her to the wisdom of the potato and helped her find peace and growth within.

Potato Chants:
To make meditation even quirkier, **Yogi Potato** introduced Pam to "Potato Chants." These were simple, repetitive phrases she could silently recite to focus her mind and bring calmness. For example, "I am as wise as a potato," or "I am grounded like a potato."

By the end of this Lesson, Pam had not only found her inner potato but also harnessed the power of "Meditato-tion." She discovered that meditation was a spud-tacular tool for calming her mind, reducing stress, and connecting with her inner wisdom.

Now, *my friend*, it's your turn to embark on your own "Meditato-tion" adventure. With the help of **Yogi Potato** and a dash of spud-tacular mindfulness, you too can achieve a mental makeover that will bring you peace, clarity, and a profound connection with your inner potato wisdom.

The journey continues with more potato-inspired mindfulness and whimsy!

Lesson 7:
Munch Your Way to Healing:
A Potato's Guide to Nutrition

As Pam's quest for personal transformation continued, she realized that nourishing her body was an essential part of the journey. This Lesson was all about embracing the wisdom of the potato to create a healthy, spud-tacular diet that would support her healing and newfound energy.

Pam's potato-nutrition guru was

"Nutri-Spud,"

a knowledgeable tuber who had spent centuries exploring the world of nutrition. **Nutri-Spud** was not only an expert in potato cuisine but also an advocate for a balanced and wholesome diet.

The Mighty Potato:
Pam began her nutrition journey with **Nutri-Spud's** golden rule: "Start with the mighty potato!"
Nutri-Spud explained that potatoes were packed with essential nutrients like vitamin C, potassium, and fibre. She learned that potatoes were not just delicious but also a cornerstone of a nutritious diet.

A Rainbow of Veggies:
Nutri-Spud introduced Pam to the concept of "eating the rainbow." Just as a bag of Skittles was colourful, a plate filled with a variety of vegetables was packed with vitamins and minerals. Pam embraced a diverse, spud-tacular array of veggies to keep her diet interesting and healthy.

Balanced Spudtrition:
Nutri-Spud encouraged Pam to find balance in her diet. She learned to include protein sources, like beans and tofu, to complement her potato dishes. The potato, after all, was a versatile canvas for creating nourishing meals.

Potato Wisdom:
Pam found that the potato was not just a humble side dish; it could also take centre stage as the main course. **Nutri-Spud** shared spud-inspired recipes that were both tasty and nutritious, from potato salad to sweet potato fries.

By the end of this Lesson, Pam had not only embraced the wisdom of the potato but had also transformed her diet into a healing and spud-tacular culinary journey.

Now, *my friend*, it's your turn to munch your way to healing, guided by the wisdom of **Nutri-Spud**. With a colourful plate, balanced spudtition, and creative potato dishes, you too can nourish your body in a way that supports your healing and newfound energy.

The journey continues with more quirky potato-inspired nutrition and whimsy!

Lesson 8:
Spud Squats and Potato Planks:
Spud-tacular Movement

With her newfound nutrition knowledge in her spudtacular arsenal, Pam was ready to take the next step in her transformation journey: embracing movement. And what better way to do it than with the guidance of

"Spud Fit,"

the quirky fitness potato with a penchant for turning exercise into a playful adventure.

Spud Squats:
Spud Fit started Pam's fitness journey with a hearty round of "Spud Squats." These exercises were inspired by the potato's natural digging instincts and involved lowering her body like she was digging for treasure. It was a quirky way to strengthen her legs and core while connecting with the earthiness of the potato.

Potato Planks:
For core strength, **Spud Fit** introduced Pam to "Potato Planks." In this quirky exercise, Pam imagined herself as a sturdy, unwavering potato, holding her body in a straight line like a plank. With every second, she could feel her core growing stronger, just like the heart of a potato.

Tater Tot Twists:
To add an element of fun to her workouts, **Spud Fit** taught Pam the "Tater Tot Twists." These were dynamic twisting exercises that reminded Pam of the whimsical way a potato could roll. With each twist, she could feel her spine becoming more flexible and her sense of playfulness returning.

Mash Your Way to Cardio:
To get her heart pumping, **Spud Fit** encouraged Pam to "Mash Her Way to Cardio." This involved rhythmic movements like mashing a potato while jumping or dancing. It was a unique and quirky way to improve her cardiovascular health and have a potato-inspired blast at the same time.

By the end of this Lesson, Pam had not only learned to appreciate exercise in a fun way but had also gained a newfound connection with her body and the playful spirit of the potato.

Now, *my friend*, it's your turn to embrace spud-tacular movement, guided by **Spud Fit**. Whether it's through Spud Squats, Potato Planks, Tater Tot Twists, or your own potato-inspired exercises, you can strengthen your body and boost your energy levels in a way that's both effective and fun.

The journey continues with more potato-inspired fitness and whimsy!

Lesson 9: Breathe Like a Potato: The Art of Tuberous Tranquillity

As Pam's transformation journey continued, she discovered that true wellness went beyond the physical. It was time for her to explore the "Art of Tuberous Tranquillity" with the guidance of a unique mentor:

"Zen Spud."

Zen Spud, a contemplative potato who radiated inner peace, introduced Pam to the art of mindful breathing. Just as potatoes took in nourishment from the soil, Pam was about to learn how to breathe in serenity and release tension.

Potato Breath:
Zen Spud began with "Potato Breath," a simple but powerful technique. He taught Pam to take slow, deep breaths, imagining that she was inhaling the essence of a freshly harvested potato. This practice grounded her and connected her to the earthy calm of the potato.

The Spud Count:
Zen Spud introduced "The Spud Count" to help Pam focus on her breath. She counted her breaths up to ten, then started over. The goal was to keep her mind centred on her breathing, just as a potato stays rooted in the soil.

Tater Tot Time:
To add a playful twist, **Zen Spud** encouraged Pam to embrace "Tater Tot Time." During this practice, she inhaled deeply and exhaled while saying "Tater" on the inhale and "Tot" on the exhale. This spudful approach made mindful breathing feel like a delightful potato game.

Meditation in Mashed Potatoes:
Zen Spud showed Pam that she could meditate in her own mashed potato way. Whether sitting in her potato pose or during her morning meal, she could take a moment to breathe mindfully and find tranquillity in the ordinary.

By the end of this Lesson, Pam had not only discovered the art of tuberous tranquillity but also understood that mindful breathing was a spud-tacular tool for reducing stress, improving focus, and nurturing her inner peace.

Now, *my friend*, it's your turn to embrace the "Art of Tuberous Tranquillity," guided by **Zen Spud**. With mindful breathing techniques like "Potato Breath," "The Spud Count," "Tater Tot Time," and even meditation in "Mashed potatoes", you too can find serenity in the everyday moments of life.

TATER TOT TIME

TATER TOT

The journey continues with more potato-inspired mindfulness and whimsy!

Lesson 10:
Emotion Fries:
Crispy, Crunchy Emotional Healing

In the midst of her spud-tacular transformation journey, Pam came to a significant realisation - that true healing went beyond the physical and nutritional aspects of her life. Emotions played a crucial role in her well-being, and it was time to dive into the world of "Emotion Fries" guided by

"Feelings Fry,"

a potato with a knack for emotional healing.

The Potato Eater's Diary:
Feelings Fry encouraged Pam to start keeping a "Potato Eater's Diary." In this fun journal, Pam recorded her daily experiences, emotions, and thoughts. Just like a potato grew in layers, the diary allowed her to peel back her emotional layers and gain insight into her feelings.

The Fry Method:
Feelings Fry introduced Pam to "The Fry Method," a technique inspired by the crispy, crunchy goodness of French fries. It involved identifying her emotional "ingredients" - the thoughts, beliefs, and past experiences that flavoured her emotions. By acknowledging and understanding these ingredients, she could take control of her emotional recipe.

The Spud Support Group:
To add a fun and communal element, **Feelings Fry** encouraged Pam to join a "Spud Support Group." This was a group of like-minded individuals on their own journeys of emotional healing. Sharing stories and insights with fellow "Potato Eaters" helped Pam realise she wasn't alone in her emotional struggles.

Fry Away Technique:
When Pam faced overwhelming emotions, **Feelings Fry** taught her the "Fry Away Technique." Just as one might release a French fry into the frying oil, Pam learned to visualise her emotions drifting away like a crispy, golden fry. This technique provided a quick and effective way to release pent-up emotions.

By the end of this Lesson, Pam had not only embraced the concept of "Emotion Fries" but had also discovered that emotional healing was as important as any other aspect of her transformation journey.

Now, *my friend*, it's your turn to explore the world of "Emotion Fries," guided by **Feelings Fry**. Through the "Potato Eater's Diary," "The Fry Method," "Spud Support Groups," and the "Fry Away Technique," you can gain a deeper understanding of your emotions and work towards emotional healing in a fun and supportive way.

The journey continues with more potato-inspired emotional wisdom and whimsy!

Lesson 11:
Spud-uality: Finding Zen in Potato Zeniths

Pam's transformation journey was taking her to new heights, both in her understanding of herself and her connection with the world. In this Lesson, she delved into the world of "Spud-uality," guided by her quirky mentor,

"Zen Potato."

The Zen Potato's Garden:
Zen Potato, a potato with a serene aura, had a unique garden where he cultivated wisdom, compassion, and inner peace. Pam was invited to stroll through this enchanted garden, filled with rows of potato plants, each representing a different aspect of spud-uality.

The Soil of Mindfulness:
Zen Potato shared that spud-uality began with the soil of mindfulness. He taught Pam to become aware of her thoughts, feelings, and sensations as if they were seeds planted in the fertile ground of her mind. Through mindful observation, she could nurture her inner garden.

The Water of Compassion:
Just as potatoes needed water to grow, **Zen Potato** explained that compassion was the nourishing element of spud-uality. Pam learned to treat herself and others with kindness, empathy, and forgiveness, watering the roots of her spiritual growth.

Harvesting Presence:
Zen Potato encouraged Pam to embrace the practice of "Harvesting Presence." This was about being fully present in each moment, savouring the richness of life, and connecting with the world around her, much like a potato drawing nourishment from the earth.

The Potato of Oneness:
In the heart of the garden, **Zen Potato** revealed the "Potato of Oneness." He explained that spud-uality was about recognising the interconnectedness of all living things, just as potatoes were connected to the soil. Pam felt a profound sense of unity with the world.

By the end of this Lesson, Pam had not only explored the depths of spud-uality but had also found a sense of peace and interconnectedness that enriched her transformation journey.

Now, *my friend*, it's your turn to uncover the world of "Spud-uality," guided by **Zen Potato**. Whether you take mindful walks, practice compassionate self-care, or simply embrace the presence of each moment, you can cultivate a deeper sense of inner peace and connection with the world.

The journey continues with more quirky potato-inspired spiritual wisdom and whimsy!

Lesson 12:
Tater's Toolkit:
Whacky Healing Wonders

As Pam's transformation journey continued, she discovered that there were countless tools and techniques she could use to enhance her well-being. In this Lesson, she delved into her **"Tater's Toolkit"** and was introduced to a range of quirky yet effective

"Whacky Healing Wonders."

The Potato Pillow:
Pam's toolkit started with the "Potato Pillow." She learned that placing a warm, potato-shaped pillow on her body could ease tension and provide comfort. It was a quirky but soothing way to relax and heal.

The Laughter Tuber:
Pam was introduced to the "Laughter Tuber," a tuber-shaped stress ball that, when squeezed, emitted joyous laughter. Pam found that just a few squeezes could lighten her mood and reduce stress, making it a spud-tacular tool for emotional healing.

The Potato Prism:
Pam discovered the "Potato Prism," a crystal-like potato that refracted and radiated positive energy. She learned how to use it for meditation and focus, basking in the quirky yet calming energy it emitted.

Spud-Scents Aromatherapy:
Pam explored "Spud-Scents Aromatherapy," a collection of potato-inspired essential oils. She learned that these unique scents, like "Potato Patchouli" and "Yam-y Lavender," could create a calming atmosphere and promote relaxation.

The Potato Puzzler:
In her toolkit, Pam found the "Potato Puzzler," a jigsaw puzzle with a potato-themed twist. She realized that working on this puzzle was a playful way to enhance her focus and mental clarity, providing a break from stress.

By the end of this Lesson, Pam had a collection of whacky healing wonders at her disposal, each contributing to her transformation journey in a fun and unique way.

Now, *my friend*, it's your turn to explore your

"Tater's Toolkit"

and embrace the whacky healing wonders within. Whether it's the
Potato Pillow,
Laughter Tuber,
Potato Prism,
Spud-Scents Aromatherapy, or the
Potato Puzzler,
these tools can add a touch of fun and relaxation to your journey of healing and well-being.

The adventure continues with more quirky potato-inspired wellness and whimsy!

Lesson 13:
Potato in the Park:
A Picnic with Nature

As Pam's transformation journey continued, she learned the importance of connecting with nature and the healing wonders it offered. In this Lesson, she embarked on a whimsical adventure, guided by

"Natura-Tater,"

a wise potato with a deep love for the great outdoors.

Potato's Nature Hike:
Natura-Tater invited Pam on a "Potato's Nature Hike." Together, they strolled through lush forests, wandered along babbling brooks, and explored meadows. Pam was amazed at how the simple act of immersing herself in nature could rejuvenate her spirit.

The Potato Picnic:
In the heart of the park, **Natura-Tater** set up a picnic like no other. They enjoyed a feast of potato-inspired dishes amidst the natural beauty, surrounded by chirping birds and rustling leaves. Pam found that dining in nature added a delightful twist to her culinary journey.

Meditation by the Creek:
Natura-Tater guided Pam in "Meditation by the Creek." They sat beside a gently flowing stream, focusing on the water's calming rhythm. The sounds of nature became a tranquil backdrop, and Pam felt her mind and spirit align with the peacefulness of the park.

Potato Artistry:
Pam discovered her artistic side with "Potato Artistry." She used the natural surroundings as her canvas and gathered leaves, twigs, and stones to create beautiful, ephemeral artworks. This creative process helped her express herself and connect with the environment.

The Spud Stroll:
Natura-Tater introduced Pam to "The Spud Stroll," a practice where she walked barefoot on the grass, connecting with the Earth's energy. Pam found this simple act of grounding to be both invigorating and calming.

By the end of this Lesson, Pam had not only embraced the healing power of nature but had also integrated it into her transformation journey as a regular source of inspiration and rejuvenation.

Now, *my friend*, it's your turn to embark on a "Potato in the Park" adventure guided by **Natura-Tater**. Whether it's a nature hike, a picnic, meditation, potato artistry, or the Spud Stroll, you can find a deeper connection with the natural world and incorporate its healing wonders into your journey of well-being and transformation.

The adventure continues with more quirky nature-inspired wellness and whimsy!

Lesson 14:
Friendship Fries: How to Ketchup and Heal

As Pam's transformation journey continued, she realised that the power of friendship was a vital ingredient in her recipe for well-being. In this Lesson, Pam embarked on a journey of "Friendship Fries," guided by

"Buddy Tater,"

a potato who specialised in cultivating and cherishing meaningful connections.

Tater Ties:
Buddy Tater introduced Pam to the concept of "Tater Ties." Just as potatoes grew best when they had strong roots in the soil, friendships thrived when they were grounded in trust and shared experiences. Pam reflected on her current relationships and those she wanted to nurture.

Spud Socials:
Pam and **Buddy Tater** attended "Spud Socials" - quirky gatherings where people shared their interests and passions. Pam realized that engaging in activities she loved was an excellent way to make new friends who shared her enthusiasm.

Ketchup Conversations:
Buddy Tater showed Pam the magic of "Ketchup Conversations." These were heart-to-heart talks where friends shared their thoughts, feelings, and experiences. Pam discovered that opening up and truly listening helped her deepen her connections.

Friendship Fries:
The highlight of this Lesson was making "Friendship Fries" with friends old and new. Pam and **Buddy Tater** hosted a spud-tacular potato-themed dinner party, where laughter and heartfelt moments were shared over delicious dishes. Pam found that such gatherings created lasting memories and strengthened bonds.

Potato Promises:
As a finale, **Buddy Tater** introduced "Potato Promises." These were simple but meaningful commitments friends made to support each other. Pam realised that building trust through small, heartfelt gestures could strengthen the roots of her friendships.

By the end of this Lesson, Pam had not only celebrated the value of her current friendships but had also welcomed new connections into her life, understanding that they were a crucial part of her journey to healing and well-being.

Now, *my friend*, it's your turn to explore the world of "Friendship Fries," guided by **Buddy Tater**. Whether you're nurturing existing friendships or cultivating new ones, remember that "ketchup conversations," "shared activities," "Potato promises," and meaningful gatherings can all play a significant role in your journey of well-being and transformation.

The adventure continues with more quirky friendship-inspired wellness and whimsy!

Lesson 15: Mashed Missions: Uncovering Your Life's Butter Purpose

Pam's transformation journey had brought her to a pivotal moment of self-discovery. In this Lesson, she delved into the world of "Mashed Missions," guided by the wise

"Mission Spud,"

a potato with a profound sense of purpose.

The Potato Vision:
Mission Spud introduced Pam to the concept of a "Potato Vision." Just as a potato grew towards the sun, she learned that having a clear vision for her life was essential. Pam contemplated her dreams and aspirations, envisioning her life's purpose.

Soulful Seasoning:
Mission Spud taught Pam about "Soulful Seasoning." This was the idea that life's challenges and experiences added flavour and depth to her journey. She realised that even the most challenging moments had contributed to her growth and purpose.

The Butter of Passion:
Pam discovered the "Butter of Passion," a unique source of motivation and joy. **Mission Spud** emphasised the importance of aligning her life's purpose with her deepest passions. She realised that pursuing what she loved brought fulfilment and a sense of purpose.

Spud Service:
Mission Spud introduced Pam to "Spud Service," a practice where she dedicated her time and talents to helping others. Pam learned that acts of kindness and service not only enriched her own life but also contributed to her sense of purpose.

Mashed Moments:
Pam embarked on a journey of "Mashed Moments." These were experiences where she felt truly alive, moments that resonated with her heart and soul. By reflecting on these times, she could uncover the breadcrumbs leading to her life's buttery purpose.

By the end of this Lesson, Pam had not only explored the depth of her own potential but also discovered the unique combination of ingredients that made up her life's buttery purpose.

Now, *my friend*, it's your turn to explore "Mashed Missions," guided by **Mission Spud**. Whether you're crafting your potato vision, embracing life's challenges, seasoning it with passion, engaging in spud service, or cherishing mashed moments, you can uncover your life's buttery purpose and embark on a journey of fulfilment and meaningful existence.

The adventure continues with more purpose-inspired wellness and whimsy!

Lesson 16:
Heal and Peel:
Potato's Guide to Creative Cuisine

Pam's transformation journey had led her to a deeper appreciation for the role of food in her well-being. In this Lesson, she delved into the world of "Heal and Peel," guided by the culinary expert

"Chef Tuber,"

a potato with an extraordinary talent for creative cuisine.

The Potato Palette:
Chef Tuber began by introducing Pam to the "Potato Palette." Just as an artist starts with a blank canvas, she learned that the potato could be a versatile canvas for creative and nutritious dishes. Pam realized that the possibilities were as endless as her imagination.

Spud Fusion:
Pam explored the concept of "Spud Fusion" - blending the culinary traditions of different cultures with the humble potato. **Chef Tuber** encouraged her to experiment with ingredients from around the world to create unique, global-inspired dishes.

The Nutrient Symphony:
Chef Tuber emphasized the importance of a "Nutrient Symphony" - creating meals that were not only delicious but also packed with essential nutrients. Pam learned that every ingredient in her dish played a role, like the notes in a beautiful melody.

Tater Artistry:
Pam dabbled in "Tater Artistry," where she used various cutting and cooking techniques to turn her dishes into edible works of art. **Chef Tuber's** guidance led her to create visually stunning and mouthwatering potato masterpieces.

Foodie Fusion Fiesta:
The highlight of this Lesson was the "Foodie Fusion Fiesta," a quirky and delicious event hosted by Pam and **Chef Tuber**. Friends and family gathered to taste her creative potato creations, from sweet potato sushi rolls to curry-spiced potato tacos.

By the end of this Lesson, Pam had not only embraced creative cuisine but had also discovered the joy of experimenting with ingredients, flavours, and presentation, making her culinary journey a source of healing and delight.

Now, *my friend,* it's your turn to explore the world of "Heal and Peel," guided by **Chef Tuber**. Whether you're working with the potato palette, embracing spud fusion, orchestrating a nutrient symphony, trying your hand at tater artistry, or hosting your own foodie fusion fiesta, creative cuisine can be a delightful and nourishing part of your journey toward well-being and transformation.

The adventure continues with more quirky and culinary-inspired wellness and whimsy!

Lesson 17:
Baked Battles and Fried Fiascos: Overcoming Challenges

Pam's journey of transformation had been a delightful adventure so far, but she was no stranger to challenges. In this Lesson, Pam faced her "Baked Battles and Fried Fiascos" with determination and resilience, guided by

"Resilient Russet,"

a potato who had mastered the art of navigating life's ups and downs.

Potato Peel Parable:
Resilient Russet shared the "Potato Peel Parable" with Pam. Just as the potato's true essence was hidden beneath its peel, she learned that her inner strength could shine through adversity. Pam began to see challenges as opportunities for growth.

The Crunchy Crisis:
Pam encountered what **Resilient Russet** called "The Crunchy Crisis." These were unexpected setbacks that could be as crunchy as a delicious crunchy crisp. With **Resilient Russet's** guidance, Pam discovered that resilience was about bouncing back from these "Crunchy Crisis" emerging stronger.

Fried Failures:
Pam faced "Fried Failures," moments when her endeavours didn't turn out as planned. **Resilient Russet** reminded her that even in failure, there were valuable lessons to be learned. Just as a fried potato was delicious, Pam's life could be enriched by her experiences, successful or not.

Potato Power Positivity:
Resilient Russet encouraged Pam to harness "Potato Power Positivity." She learned that maintaining a positive mindset and focusing on her strengths could help her persevere through difficult times. The potato's unwavering growth in any soil became an inspiring symbol of resilience.

Mashed Magic:
Pam discovered "Mashed Magic," the transformation that could come from facing adversity head-on. She realised that, just like a potato mashed and seasoned, she could emerge from challenges with newfound wisdom, humility, and strength.

By the end of this Lesson, Pam had not only overcome her "Baked Battles and Fried Fiascos" but had also embraced her inner resilience as a vital part of her transformation journey.

Now, *my friend*, it's your turn to face your own "Baked Battles and Fried Fiascos," guided by **Resilient Russet**. Whether you're navigating potato peel moments, handling crunchy crises, overcoming fried failures, embracing potato power positivity, or discovering mashed magic, **Resilient Russet** can be your spud-tacular companion in the journey of well-being and transformation.

The adventure continues with more fun and life-inspired wellness and wisdom!

Lesson 18:
Spud Rituals:
Tuber-Therapy for Everyday Life

As Pam's journey of transformation continued, she recognised the need for daily practices that could bring calm and mindfulness into her life. In this Lesson, she explored the world of "Spud Rituals" guided by

"Ritual Tater,"

a potato who had a knack for turning everyday moments into therapeutic experiences.

Morning Mashing:
Ritual Tater introduced Pam to "Morning Mashing." Just as a potato was mashed to create a fresh start, Pam began her day with a simple morning ritual. She mashed her thoughts of yesterday to create a clean mental slate for the day ahead.

Potato Pause:
Pam embraced the "Potato Pause," a practice where she took a moment to pause and connect with her breath. Just as a potato paused in the soil to gather nutrients, Pam found that this simple practice allowed her to gather her thoughts and regain focus.

Spud Scent Meditation:
Ritual Tater encouraged Pam to practice "Spud Scent Meditation." She used potato-inspired scents, like "Potato Patchouli" or "Yam-y Lavender," to create a soothing atmosphere. This unique form of aromatherapy helped her relax and find peace.

Potato Reflections:
Pam started "Potato Reflections," in her "Spud Journal", a daily journaling ritual. She used her journal to reflect on her experiences, express gratitude, and set intentions for the future. Much like a potato grows, Pam's thoughts and reflections evolved over time.

Spud Sleep Time:
At the end of the day, Pam practiced "Spud Sleep Time." She created a calming bedtime routine, incorporating potato-themed elements like a potato-shaped pillow or potato-scented candles. This routine helped her unwind and drift into restful sleep.

By the end of this Lesson, Pam had not only embraced "Spud Rituals" but also discovered that simple daily practices could infuse her life with mindfulness, relaxation, and a sense of well-being.

Now, *my friend*, it's your turn to explore the world of "Spud Rituals," guided by **Ritual Tater**. Whether you're starting with morning mashing, taking a potato pause, practicing spud scent meditation, engaging in potato reflections, or winding down with spud sleep time, these daily rituals can add a touch of mindfulness and serenity to your journey of well-being and transformation.

The adventure continues with more quirky and therapeutic-inspired wellness and whimsy!

Lesson 19: Potato Gratitude: Give Thanks, Not Starches

As Pam's journey of transformation continued, she realised the importance of gratitude in shaping her mindset and well-being. In this Lesson, she delved into the world of "Potato Gratitude" guided by

"Grateful Spud,"

a potato with a heart full of appreciation and a quirky approach to practicing gratitude.

Spudful Start:
Grateful Spud introduced Pam to the concept of a "Spudful Start." Instead of filling her thoughts with starchy concerns, Pam began each day with a heart full of appreciation. She greeted the morning with gratitude for the simple joys of life.

Tater Blessings:
Pam counted her "Tater Blessings." **Grateful Spud** encouraged her to create a list of the people, experiences, and things she was thankful for. This practice allowed Pam to realise the abundance of blessings in her life.

The Spud Journal:
Pam maintained a "Spud Journal" where she recorded her daily potato-themed moments of gratitude. This beautiful journal was filled with entries about simple joys, like a heart-shaped potato she found or a friendly chat with a neighbour.

Potato Picnics of Gratitude:
Pam embraced the idea of "Potato Picnics of Gratitude." These were impromptu picnics with friends or by herself, where she enjoyed potato-themed dishes and celebrated the abundance of life. These picnics were a reminder that gratitude could be a joyful and shared experience.

Random Acts of Tuber-ness:
Grateful Spud inspired Pam to perform "Random Acts of Tuber-ness." These were small, unexpected acts of kindness she carried out for friends and strangers, spreading gratitude and happiness throughout her community.

By the end of this Lesson, Pam had not only embraced "Potato Gratitude" but had also discovered that practicing gratitude was a delightful way to shift her focus toward the positive aspects of life.

Now, *my friend*, it's your turn to explore the world of "Potato Gratitude," guided by **Grateful Spud**. Whether you're starting with a spudful start, counting your tater blessings, keeping a spud journal, enjoying potato picnics of gratitude, or engaging in random acts of tuber-ness, these practices can infuse your life with positivity, appreciation, and a sense of well-being.

The adventure continues with more gratitude-inspired wellness and whimsy!

Lesson 20: From Spud to Superhero: Your Healing Journey Continues

Pam's transformation journey had been a fantastic adventure filled with insights, experiences, and newfound wisdom. In this final Lesson, she realised that her journey was an ongoing quest to become her own superhero. Pam was ready to step into her role as the

"Super Spud"

of her own life, and she did so with a sense of quirky determination.

Embrace Your Inner Super Spud:
Pam understood that, just like potatoes had unique qualities and strengths, she too possessed remarkable qualities that made her a **Super Spud**. Whether it was resilience, kindness, creativity, or determination, she recognised her inner superhero qualities.

Spudtacular Super Powers:
Pam identified her "Spudtacular Super Powers." These were her unique talents and abilities that she could use to navigate life's challenges and bring positivity to the world. Whether it was her sense of humour or her compassion, she harnessed these powers for good.

Potato Positivity in Action:
Pam put her "Potato Positivity in Action." She practiced spreading positivity by sharing her journey and helping others find their own path to well-being. She realised that by being a beacon of light, she could inspire others to embark on their healing journeys.

The Super Spud Community:
Pam became part of the "Super Spud Community," a fun and supportive group of individuals who had embarked on their own journeys of transformation. Together, they shared their experiences, celebrated each other's successes, and faced challenges as a united team.

Spud Blessings:
Pam's journey concluded with a practice of "Spud Blessings." She took a moment each day to reflect on the abundance of blessings in her life, both big and small. This practice reminded her to continue embracing gratitude and appreciation as her superpowers.

By the end of this Lesson, Pam had not only embraced her role as the **"Super Spud"** of her own life but had also discovered that the journey of healing and well-being was an ongoing adventure filled with endless possibilities.

Now, *my friend*, it's your turn to become the

"Super Spud"

of your own life. Embrace your inner superhero qualities, recognise your spudtacular superpowers, put potato positivity into action, find your own community of support, and continue counting your spud blessings. Your journey of healing and well-being is a continuous adventure, and you have the power to make it as fun as you desire.

The journey continues with you as the superhero of your own story!

Printed in Great Britain
by Amazon